Living Jewish Values

VOLUME 1: BE YOUR BEST SELF

VOLUME 2: FAMILY CONNECTIONS

Teacher's Lesson Plan Manual

By Rabbi Miriam T. Spitzer

36 Ready-to-Use Lesson Plans

Project Editor: Mark H. Levine
Design: AURAS Design

Springfield, New Jersey
ISBN: 978-0-87441-871-2

Behrman House, Inc.
www.behrmanhouse.com

Contents

Introduction

TEACHING JEWISH VALUES

When we say "the Torah," we generally mean either the Torah scroll made of parchment that we take out of the *Aron Kodesh* (Holy Ark), or the content of the scroll that we find in the *Chumash.* But sometimes the word "Torah" is used to mean the expanse of Jewish holy texts, including the Torah, the rest of the *Tanakh,* the Talmud, the Midrash, liturgy, and the sermons that our rabbi gives every Shabbat.

In this broader sense, Jewish values are very much part of Torah. Our Jewish values are the morals, principles, and ethics by which we choose to live our lives. The study and teaching of these values are part of the mitzvah (yes, the value) of *Talmud Torah,* learning and teaching Torah. The *Living Jewish Values* volumes come to help us with the *Talmud Torah* of Jewish values.

The first volume of the *Living Jewish Values* series focuses on the self; the second volume focuses on the family. Students learn in different ways, and different values will resonate for each person. The book presents each value from many perspectives and with many facets in order to enrich the learning experience. May using this book help you and your students find meaning through engaging with Jewish values.

USING THIS LESSON PLAN MANUAL

This lesson plan manual offers the teacher ready-made lesson plans to use or to adapt to maximize potential of the *Living Jewish Values* volumes. The lessons are designed to run approximately 50 minutes, though you may choose to have some run longer or shorter. Many lessons incorporate art and other projects, and teachers should be sure to gather materials in advance.

Each opening activity is preceded by a **"POSTER BOARD QUESTION."** This question should be written on the board or easel before the students come in for the lesson. When the students arrive, along with taking off their coats, getting out their books, and having a snack, part of the settling in process should include writing an answer to the "poster board question" while sitting at their desks. The questions offered here are related to what will be discussed in class that day and will help get the students thinking. The poster board questions are not intended to be directly discussed or referred to during class.

STRUCTURE OF THE LESSON PLAN

Each lesson plan includes the following components:

- **Essential Question.** The overarching question of the lesson, usually an open-ended question that lends itself to many different answers and to repeated examination over the course of a lifetime.
- **Learning Objectives.** A list of three main goals that the students will achieve by the end of the lesson.
- **Getting Started.** An opening activity, discussion or song that "hooks" the student in and sets the scene for what will follow, preceded by a "**poster board question.**"
- **Exploring the Text.** Using the text in the book (and occasionally other texts) to introduce and explore the Jewish value. Often includes discussion topics relating to, but not identical to, what is in the book.

- **Experiential Learning.** Opportunities for students to learn by doing. Activities may include art projects, games, quizzes, skits, etc.—some from within the textbook, and others not.
- **Wrapping It Up.** A conclusion to the lesson, offering an opportunity to review and reflect on what was learned.
- **Home–School Connection.** An activity to do at home, designed to share with families the values and lessons learned at school. Sometimes this will be a discussion to have over the dinner table, sometimes a quiz to do together with family members, sometimes a more elaborate activity to do at home.

SETTING THE SCENE

We have a textbook to teach Jewish values, but we are teaching Jewish values also and always through the examples that we set for our students. The mood we set in our classroom, the *derekh eretz* (common courtesy) expectations, the relationships we build, are at least as important as the material we are teaching. Our classroom should be a model of encouragement, acceptance, and mutual respect. Many classes find it useful to have a class *brit,* or set of expectations. Students should be expected to work together and support each other.

USE OF TECHNOLOGY

Technology offers a myriad of opportunities for enriching the learning experience. You Tube videos and other Web sites are utilized throughout the lesson plan manual to increase the excitement and interactivity of the lessons. Even if you cannot access the Internet in your classroom, CDs can be played to provide music, and information and pictures can often be printed in advance to distribute to the students.

Technology is often an excellent tool to enhance learning, but it should not be a goal in and of itself. Please keep Internet safety in mind and send students only to Web sites you have previously vetted and approved.

DIFFERENTIATED INSTRUCTION

Children, like adults, learn in a variety of ways. Some students learn best by reading aloud, some by reading silently, and some by hearing the words read to them. Some students are visual learners, some auditory learners, and some kinesthetic learners. Some students learn best in groups and some prefer to work alone. But all learners gain from having opportunities to learn in multiple ways and to reinforce what they are doing in multiple formats.

When we teach, we want both to encourage children to work to their strengths and to encourage children to try new things and explore new areas. Fourth and fifth grade is too young to declare "I am not good at that" or "I am only good at this." In these lesson plans, students are given opportunities to learn in many different ways, both within lessons and between lessons. There are opportunities for reading silently and reading aloud, for dramatic play-acting, for drawing, for analytical writing and creative writing, and students should try them all over the course of the year.

Most of the lessons vary activities at least every 15 minutes or so. Doing this will keep children interested and involved in what is going on. Every lesson plan also includes at least one opportunity for **Experiential Learning**, meaning that students learn by doing. Such activities include quizzes, games, skits, art projects, creative writing, poetry writing, and more.

GROUP WORK

One principle of the religious school classroom should be that everyone works with everyone. We teach Jewish values not only through the text, but also through the examples we set. While it might be tempting to place students who work well together in the same group, doing so will ultimately prevent students from developing the skills they need to work with all sorts of people. Teachers should make sure that over the course of time, everyone works with everyone: boys with girls, louder students with quieter students, strong readers with weaker readers, and so forth.

At the beginning of the year, teachers should establish clear rules and expectations for group work. For example, students should be expected to speak with indoor voices and to remain within their groups. You may find it useful to have a delineation of jobs within the groups, so every student knows what his or her job is that day. (Note that not every job is necessarily applicable to every group work assignment.) Some possible jobs could include:

- Recorder: Takes notes of the group's discussions and ideas.
- Reporter: Reports the group's work to the class.
- Illustrator: Draws the group's ideas.
- Reader: Reads aloud to the group.
- Encourager: Encourages group members to stay on task.

LIVING JEWISH VALUES

PART 1

Lesson Plans for Volume 1: Be Your Best Self

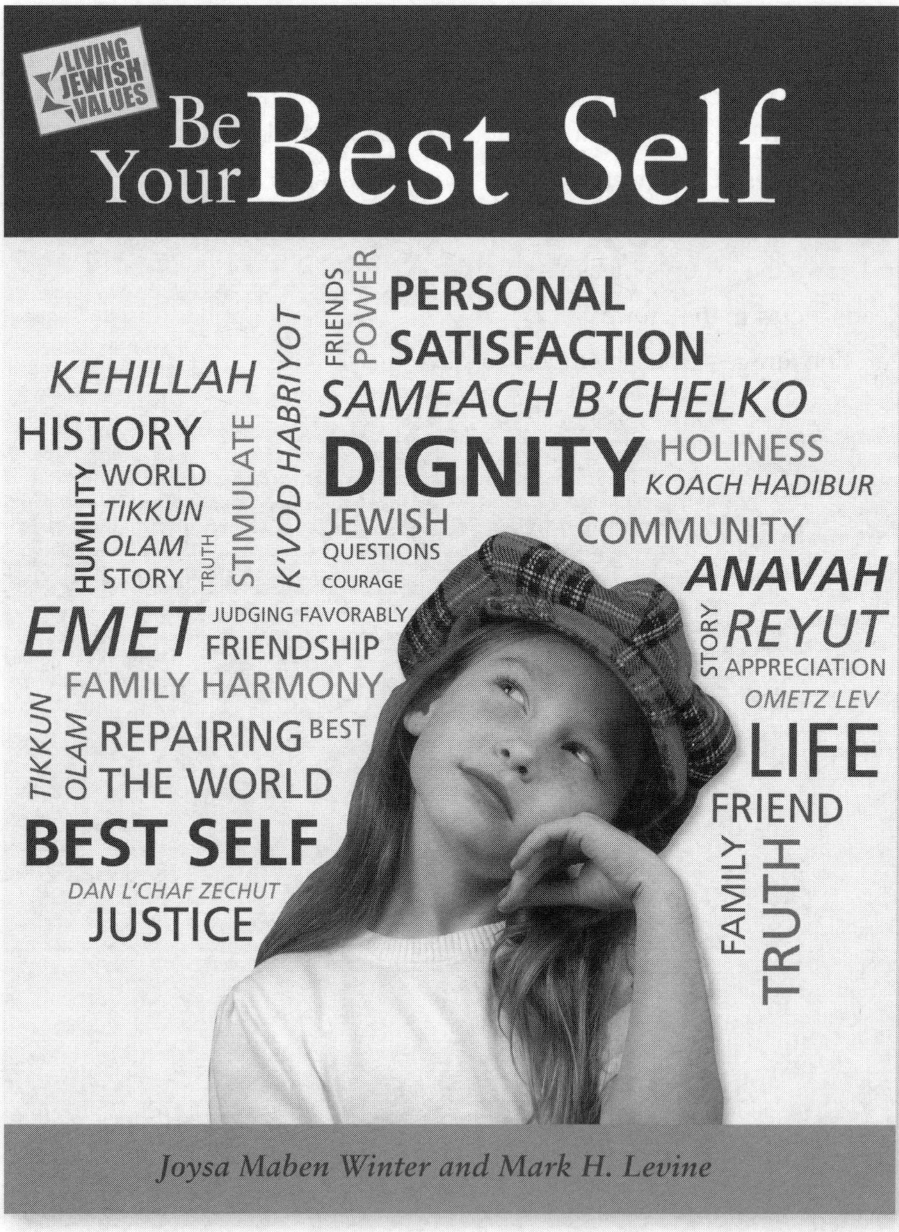

LESSON PLANS FOR VOLUME 1: BE YOUR BEST SELF

Introduction

The *Living Jewish Values* series introduces some of the most important—and sustaining—values of our tradition. In this first volume, *Be Your Best Self*, we examine four values that underlie personal enrichment and growth:

- *K'vod Habriyot* (Individual Dignity)
- *T'Shuvah* Returning to Your Best Self)
- *Sameach B'chelko* (Personal Satisfaction)
- *Anavah* (Humility)

Each chapter introduces the value to the students, shows how the value resonated in Jewish history, presents an inspiring model for the students to emulate, and gives them ways to incorporate the value into their own lives. This lesson plan manual offers the teacher ready-made lesson plans to use or to adapt to help facilitate the teaching of these values. There are three lesson plans for each value, each with its own learning objectives and its own essential questions. In addition, the value of *t'shuvah* is reinforced in the lesson plan for Rosh Hashanah and Yom Kippur, and the value of *sameach b'chelko* is reinforced in the lesson plan for Sukkot. The holiday lesson plans are found in the back of this manual.

ESSENTIAL QUESTIONS

	LESSON 1	LESSON 2	LESSON 3
CHAPTER 1 *K'vod Habriyot* Individual Dignity	What is *k'vod habriyot* (individual dignity)?	Is *k'vod habriyot* only about bullying and "saving face," or are there other factors involved?	How can I practice *k'vod habriyot* in my own life?
CHAPTER 2 *T'shuvah* Returning to Your Best Self	What does *t'shuvah* mean?	How have other people done *t'shuvah* in their lives?	What do I want to change in my life?
CHAPTER 3 *Sameach B'chelko* Personal Satisfaction	What does *sameach b'chelko* mean?	Can contentment lead to complacency, and is that a problem?	Is it true that those who seek more than they need hinder themselves from enjoying what they have?
CHAPTER 4 *Anavah* Humility	What is *anavah* (humility)?	How does *anavah* help the world?	How can I incorporate more *anavah* into my life?

VOLUME 1 • CHAPTER 1

K'vod Habriyot, Lesson 1 of 3

Essential Question: What is k'vod habriyot *(individual dignity)?*

Lesson Objectives: Students will be able to:

1. Define the words *k'vod habriyot* and explain what dignity means.
2. List ways to increase each student's sense of dignity in the classroom.
3. Conceive of ways to help others "save face."

Getting Started: (5 minutes)

POSTER BOARD QUESTION: What is embarrassing?

- Introduce the term *k'vod habriyot. K'vod,* from the word meaning honor or respect. *K'vod habriyot* means the dignity of the individual.
- Most classrooms have a class *brit,* or list of expectations. Review this list together and ask: Which of these commitments we made have to do with the dignity of the students in the classroom? Mark the ones that do. (In the unlikely case that none do, revise the class *brit* so that it does address *k'vod habriyot.*)

Exploring the Text: (20 minutes)

- Read the first story aloud to the class.
- Divide the class in half. Have half the students read the rest of the introduction individually and do the "Stamp Out Bullying" page (Activity 1). Have the other half of the class read the Carlebach page and answer the "Saving Face" questions (Activity 2).
- **Group sharing:** Activity 1 group should present its solutions to bullying and why Rabbi Eliezer's advice is helpful. Activity 2 group should explain what "saving face" means, and tell how to work to help others save face.

Experiential Learning: (15 minutes)

TIME CAPSULE: EXPLORING *K'VOD HABRIYOT* IN HISTORY

Read the question(s) aloud and have students, either individually or in pairs, respond to one of the questions. Answers should be printed neatly because these will be used for one of the panels on the class *k'vod habriyot* mural (see Lesson 3).

Wrapping It Up: (5–10 minutes)

Review what *k'vod habriyot* means. Talk about ways we can increase *k'vod habriyot* in the classroom. Brainstorm ways we can present these ideas in a visual fashion to remind ourselves and others around us of the important concept of *k'vod habriyot.*

Home–School Connection

Assign the "Do you treat people with dignity?" personality quiz for homework, including doing the quiz and taking it to the dinner table for family discussion.

VOLUME 1 • CHAPTER 1

K'vod Habriyot, Lesson 2 of 3

Essential Question: Is k'vod habriyot *only about bullying and "saving face," or are there other factors involved?*

Lesson Objectives: Students will be able to:

1. Identify Rose Schneiderman and discuss what she accomplished.
2. Give examples of other people who searched for systemic solutions to dignity problems.
3. Talk about different aspects of *k'vod habriyot,* including how we treat others in the classroom, and how society treats different groups within it.

Getting Started: (5–7 minutes)

POSTER BOARD QUESTION: Who are your heroes?

- Give students an opportunity to report on their responses and their family conversation about the "Do you treat people with dignity?" quiz that they did for homework. Ask what kind of "-isms" are barriers to *k'vod habriyot? (racism, anti-Semitism, ageism, elitism, etc.)*

Exploring the Text: (10–15 minutes)

- Have a student read the *K'vod Habriyot* Superstar page aloud.
- Ask the following questions (you might want to have handouts or websites available for short research opportunities):
  - Was Rose Schneiderman working to save face for the workers? *(No, she was concerned with a different dignity issue.)*
  - So what does this story have to do with *k'vod habriyot? (The abysmal working conditions clearly showed that there was no* k'vod habriyot.*)*
  - What would proper working conditions look like? *(safe conditions; reasonable hours; time for lunch, drinks, and bathroom breaks; windows in the rooms; medical insurance, etc.).*
  - What was Rose Schneiderman trying to do? *(She was trying to give workers the power to say—and get—what they needed.)*
  - Can you think of other people who worked to change the world in a way that there would be more *k'vod habriyot? [(possibilities include: Rev. Martin Luther King, Jr., Rosa Parks (racism); Temple Grandin (autism); Gloria Steinem (feminism); Moses Mendelssohn (anti-Semitism).]*

Experiential Learning: (15–20 minutes)

In small groups, have students make a small poster board about one of the people the class brainstormed above. These poster boards will be displayed together as part of the class mural (see Lesson 3).

Wrapping It Up: (5 minutes)

Let each group present its poster board and explain how the person shown increased *k'vod habriyot*.

Home–School Connection

Have students go home and ask their families whether they can identify Rose Schneiderman. If not, have the students explain to their parents who she was and what she did. Encourage students to have a family discussion on how to add *k'vod habriyot* into the world.

VOLUME 1 • CHAPTER 1

K'vod Habriyot, Lesson 3 of 3

Essential Question: How can I practice k'vod habriyot *in my own life?*

Lesson Objectives: Students will be able to:

1. Think about bullying as a dignity issue.
2. Look for opportunities to treat people with dignity.
3. Articulate the connection between greater social issues and *k'vod habriyot.*

Getting Started: (5–10 minutes)

POSTER BOARD QUESTION: Rabbi Eliezer said: "Let the dignity of others be as dear to you as your own." (Pirkei Avot 2:10) What does this mean?

- This will not be the first time the students hear this statement. After two classes of learning about *k'vod habriyot*, they will have insights into what it means. This statement will also be the centerpiece/title of the mural they will be assembling during this lesson.
- Ask and discuss: What would the world be like if everyone recognized that we are made in the image of God?

Exploring the Text: (10 minutes)

Have students individually read and write down the answers to the questions in the "What I Think" section.

Experiential Learning

Students will produce a class mural incorporating all the different facets of *k'vod habriyot* that they have been learning. While some segments of the mural may have already been made during earlier lessons, this lesson is devoted to completing the different components, assembling them, and seeing the big picture. It may take more than one class.

- Write the title of the mural, to be placed in the center: "Let the dignity of others be as dear to you as your own." (Pirkei Avot 2:10)
- Display the questions and answers from the "Time Capsule: Exploring *K'vod Habriyot* in History" activity from Lesson 1.
- Display the *K'vod Kabriyot* Superhero poster boards from Lesson 2.
- Draw and display goofus and gallant type cartoons showing how to properly express *k'vod habriyot.*
- Develop a class *brit* with an emphasis on *k'vod habriyot.*
- Encourage the students to suggest other ideas for the mural.

Wrapping It Up

Bring the class together and walk around, looking at each part of the mural and taking pride in its completion.

Home–School Connection

Invite parents in to see the class mural. Another possibility might be to take a digital photo of the mural and e-mail it to parents and/or include it in a school newsletter.

VOLUME 1 • CHAPTER 2

T'shuvah, Lesson 1 of 3

Essential Question: What does t'shuvah *mean?*

Lesson Objectives: Students will be able to:

1. Define *t'shuvah* with the classic understanding of repentance.
2. Define *t'shuvah* as returning to one's best self.
3. Consider when, if ever, it is too late to do *t'shuvah.*

Getting Started

POSTER BOARD QUESTION: When you are true to your "better self," what are you like?

- Play the song "The Book of Good Life" by the Maccabeats, found at www.youtube.com/watch?v=DRaQSbuTiBg

Exploring the Text: (5 minutes)

- Read the beginning of the chapter together as a class, including the opening *midrash* and the "Overcoming Obstacles To *T'shuvah*" section.
- Skip two pages (they will be covered in later lessons) and read the Agaddah story together.

Experiential Learning: (20-30 minutes)

AGADDIC TRADITION DEBATE

Have half the class take the position: "They had their chance. Their *t'shuvah* was too late; too bad, they blew it." Have the other half take Maimonides' position: The person who does *t'shuvah* "is beloved by the Creator … as if he or she had never erred." Give the groups 5–10 minutes to prepare their positions and list their arguments.

Have the debate:

- Flip a coin to determine who goes first.
- Each group gets 3 minutes to state its position.
- Give the groups 3 minutes to prepare a question for the other group.
- Group that went second in presentation asks the first question for the other group; 2 minutes to answer.
- Other group asks a question; 2 minutes to answer.
- Give each group another 2 minutes for a final comment.

Wrapping It Up

Bring the class back together. Ask: What does *t'shuvah* mean?

Make sure the students know that it means both repentance and returning to your best self. Tell them that during the next class they will be learning about people who did *t'shuvah* and returned to their better selves after doing some pretty bad things.

VOLUME 1 • CHAPTER 2

T'shuvah, Lesson 2 of 3

Essential Question: How have other people done t'shuvah *in their lives?*

Lesson Objectives: Students will be able to:

1. Explain what *beit t'shuvah* is and what it does.
2. Tell in detail about one person's *t'shuvah* journey.
3. Know about the *t'shuvah* journeys of a number of other people who were able to effect change in their lives and use their experiences to help others.

Getting Started: (5 minutes)

POSTER BOARD QUESTION: Can a person change his/her character, or is biology determinative? Explain.

- Ask and discuss: Do you know people who have turned their lives around?

Experiential Learning: (20 minutes)

- Go to *www.beittshuvah.wordpress.com/about* and show the class the video about *Beit T'shuvah.* (6 minutes)
- Divide the class into small groups. Each group explores a different *T'shuvah* Superstar, learns about and answers a couple of questions about that person. At the end (see Wrapping It Up), the class comes back together and each group reports on one inspirational story about the superstar it researched.
  - Read about Rabbi Mark Borowitz in the text book. What did Rabbi Mark used to be like? What is he like now? What did he do with his new life?
  - Go to *www.beittshuvah.wordpress.com/2012/01/16/i-have-a-dream* and read "I have a dream" by Erin Pad. What did Erin used to be like? What is she like now? How did she change?
  - Read about the ex-skinhead, Frank Meeink, at *www.frankmeeink.com/whois.html* and *www.harmonythroughhockey.org*. What did Frank used to be like? What is he like now? What made him change? What did he do with his new life?

Wrapping It Up: (10 minutes)

Bring the class back together. Each group has a chance to briefly report on the *T'shuvah* Superstar the group studied and something remarkable about that person. If time allows, groups should be able to ask each other questions.

Home–School Connection

Students should go home and tell their families about how their superstar changed his or her life through *t'shuvah*, and how that change helped others.

VOLUME 1 • CHAPTER 2

T'shuvah, Lesson 3 of 3

Essential Question: What do I want to change in my life?

Lesson Objectives: Students will be able to:

1. Articulate changes they want to make in themselves.
2. Be aware of obstacles to *t'shuvah.*
3. Apply principles of *t'shuvah* to their own lives.

Getting Started: (5–10 minutes)

POSTER BOARD QUESTION: Rabbi Eliezer, who said that "the *k'vod* of others should be as dear to you as your own," also said, "Repent the day before you die." What do you think this means?

- Take the "Are you on the path to *t'shuvah?*" quiz individually.

Exploring the Text: (5 minutes)

Read the "Overcoming Obstacles to *T'shuvah*" section together as a class. (They read it during Lesson 1 of this chapter; this is a focused review.)

Experiential Learning: (20–25 minutes)

- Have the students do Activity 1 individually.
- Have the students do Activity 3 individually.
- Ask the students to choose one activity from the "What I Think" section to work on over the next week. Suggest that they make a plan for how they are going to do it.

Wrapping It Up: (5–10 minutes)

Come back together as a class and encourage students to share one thing that they want to change about themselves.

Home–School Connection

Ask students to do one activity from the "What I Think" section.

Sameach B'chelko, Lesson 1 of 3

Essential Question: What does sameach b'chelko *mean?*

Lesson Objectives: Students will be able to:

1. Translate the term *sameach b'chelko* (personal satisfaction).
2. Evaluate wants vs. needs in different contexts.
3. Articulate the difference between wants and needs.

Getting Started: (3–5 minutes)

POSTER BOARD QUESTION: If you were stranded on a desert island, what would you bring with you?

- Write the term *sameach b'chelko* on the board in Hebrew. Brainstorm with the class other times they have heard the word *sameach* in that or other forms. *(chag sameach, simchat torah, simchah dancing)*

Exploring the Text: (5–10 minutes)

Read pages 22 and 23 together as a class. Have the students read page 27 individually.

Experiential Learning: (20–25 minutes)

NEEDS VS. WANTS (ACTIVITY 1, PAGE 24)

- Divide into groups of three.
- Have the students in each group open their books to page 24. Each group should consider the needs and wants of three different people and write their names at the top of the page. Label the first: "Student in my grade in this school," label the second: "for family of 6 in which one parent works at home on the computer as a graphic designer and the other parent is a doctor," and label the third: "for Dr. Rahamim Melamed-Cohen, the *Sameach b'chelko* Superstar on page 27."
- In their groups, the students should then discuss each example and draw the needs vs. wants lines to the appropriate person at the top of the page.
- Bring the class back together. Ask and discuss:
  - Are all of the needs and wants the same for all three people?
  - Are any of the needs and wants the same for all three people?
  - Can something that is a "need" for one person be a "want" for someone else?
  - Can you think of any "needs" for everyone that are not listed on this page? *(air, water, friendship, love, community)*
- Have students complete "What Turns Your Frown Upside Down" on page 25, individually.

Wrapping It Up: (5 minutes)

In Pirkei Avot it says: The more possessions, the more worries. Discuss.

VOLUME 1 • CHAPTER 3

Sameach B'chelko, Lesson 2 of 3

Essential Question: Can contentment lead to complacency, and is that a problem?

Lesson Objectives: Students will be able to:

1. Recognize the Elohai N'shama prayer.
2. See prayer as a personal inspiration.
3. Recognize that complacency is a pitfall of contentment.

Getting Started: (2 minutes)

POSTER BOARD QUESTION: What makes you happy?

- Play the Debbie Friedman "Elohai N'shama" song. If you don't have it on a CD, you can listen to it on You Tube at www.youtube.com/watch?v=BaEJKe25BPo.

Exploring the Text: (15–20 minutes)

- Have students quickly reread the story of Dr. Rachamim Melamed-Cohen on page 27.
- Provide a side-by-side copy of Elohai Netzor (can be found in *Siddur Sim Sh'lom,* page 8), and of "Kol Od" by Dr. Rachamim Melamed-Cohen (www.melamed.org.il/songsEN.html). English translation of "Kol Od": As long as my soul is within me / there is strength in my being / a smile on my lips / and around me they smile at me / as long as I can connect / and allow / friends to talk / with me / that is me. / When my time comes / take me / not at the hands of / an assistant /of flesh and blood / but You / who in the future personally take my soul / because You created it / You fashioned it / and I am happy / as long as my soul is still within me.
- Students should read both poems, compare them, and see that Dr. Melamed-Cohen used the traditional prayer as an inspiration for his personal prayer. Focus on how happy and grateful he seems, in spite of his physical condition.

Experiential Learning: (15–20 minutes)

Divide into small groups. Have the students read the story on page 26 to each other. They will probably find it both astonishing and strange. Come back together as a class. Ask the group:

- What did you think of the story?
- What are the dangers of feeling contentment regardless of the circumstances? Have a discussion about complacency. Was Dr. Melamed-Cohen content or complacent?

Wrapping It Up: (4 minutes)

Play Dr. Melamed-Cohen's song "Kol Od," found at www.melamed.org.il/songsEN.html.

VOLUME 1 • CHAPTER 3

Sameach B'chelko, Lesson 3 of 3

Essential Question: Is it true that those who seek more than they need hinder themselves from enjoying what they have?

Lesson Objectives: Students will be able to:

1. Apply the ideas of *sameach b'chelko* to their own lives.
2. Consider whether there are good reasons to make do with less.

Getting Started

POSTER BOARD QUESTION: What was the best gift you ever gave?

- Have the students work in pairs on page 30 (Activity 3).

Exploring the Text: (10–15 minutes)

- Write on the board:
  - Do you agree that people who can afford to wear fancy clothes or have fancy toys should not because it might make other people jealous?
  - Can you think of any other reasons that people should not always spend money even if they can afford to?
- Have students work individually to answer one of the two questions on pages 28 and 29 using the questions on the board as an aid. If time allows, have a class discussion and encourage students to share some of their responses.

Experiential Learning: (10–15 minutes)

Have students write a poem, song, or rap about the ideas of *sameach b'chelko* in pairs or small groups. Then have them perform the poems, songs, or raps for each other.

Wrapping It Up: (5 minutes)

Discuss: Those who seek more than they need hinder themselves from enjoying what they have.

Home–School Connection

Have students complete "What I Think" on page 31 at home with their parents.

VOLUME 1 • CHAPTER 4

Anavah, Lesson 1 of 3

Essential Question: What is anavah *(humility)?*

Lesson Objectives: Students will be able to:

1. Define *anavah* (humility).
2. Distinguish between self-esteem and *anavah*.
3. Apply *anavah* and self-esteem to regular everyday experiences.

Getting Started: (5 minutes)

POSTER BOARD QUESTION: What are you especially proud of?

- Ask the class to imagine someone who is running for office, maybe a politician, maybe a classmate running for student council. What is the difference between bragging and telling the voters why they should vote for him/her?

Exploring the Text: (5 minutes)

Read the opening sections of the *anavah* chapter together as a class.

Experiential Learning: (25 minutes)

ROLE PLAYING GAME

Parts: arrogant student, student with absolutely no confidence, student with good self-esteem, teacher.

You may decide to vary the students playing the roles in each case, or to keep the same student actors.

- Case 1. The teacher praises the student's work in front of the whole class. Act it out. Each student should react according to his/her assigned role. Offer an alternative: Did you like how the actors portrayed the students? How would you do any of them differently?
- Case 2. The teacher yells at the student in front of the whole class. Offer an alternative: Did you like how the actors portrayed the students? How would you do any of them differently?
- Case 3. The teacher takes the student aside privately and makes a suggestion for how something might be done better. Offer an alternative: Did you like how the actors portrayed the students? How would you do any of them differently?

Discuss the experience. How did the arrogant student react to being praised? To being yelled at? How did the meek student react to being praised? To being yelled at? How about the humble student with good self-esteem, how did he/she react? What can we learn from this about our reactions? What can we learn from this about how we deliver praise or rebuke?

Wrapping It Up: (5 minutes)

Read the agaddic tradition together.

Home–School Connection

Provide enough copies of "How does your light shine?" for students and their family members to each do at home.

VOLUME 1 • CHAPTER 4

Anavah, Lesson 2 of 3

Essential Question: How does anavah *improve personal relationships?*

Lesson Objective: Students will be able to:

Recognize that humility allows us to feel pride in our achievements without feeling superior to others.

Getting Started: (5 minutes)

POSTER BOARD QUESTION: Can humility be an obstacle to personal success?

- Ask the class: Who is the most humble person you know? What makes that person humble? How do you feel around him/her?
- Consider the people named. How many are famous politicians? How many are famous athletes? How many are movie stars? How many are famous scientists? How many are famous at all?

Exploring the Text: (10–15 minutes)

- Have students read *Anavah* Superstar individually. Underline the parts that show Einstein's humility.
- **Individual writing assignment:** Imagine that you met Albert Einstein coming out of the ice cream shop and he stopped to say hi to you. Write a dialogue of the conversation that might have taken place.

Experiential Learning: (10–15 minutes)

TIME CAPSULE: *ANAVAH* IN HISTORY

- In pairs, read both stories and choose the one you want to respond to.
- Write a response to the person asking the question.
- Trade responses with another group writing an answer to the same dilemma. What advice did you give that was the same? What advice did you give that was different?

Wrapping It Up: (5–10 minutes)

Class discussion: In the "What I Think" section, describe what the world would be like if all people lived by the value of humility. How might society, your school, or even your family function differently?

Home–School Connection

Collect and bring in pictures from magazines or personal photos demonstrating how you show *anavah* in your life.

VOLUME 1 • CHAPTER 4

Anavah, Lesson 3 of 3

Essential Question: How can I incorporate more anavah *into my life?*

Lesson Objectives: Students will be able to:

1. Articulate ways in which they can add *anavah* to their lives.
2. Explore excessive pride and lack of confidence to define a healthy balance of *anavah* (humility).

Getting Started: (4 minutes)

POSTER BOARD QUESTION: What are you particularly good at?

- Show the Muppets version of "Oh Lord, it is Hard to be Humble," found at www.youtube.com/watch?v=tn1Qolv4ntQ.

Experiential Learning: (40 minutes)

- **Class discussion:** Question 2 of "What I Think." Think of a time when excessive pride caused you to *overestimate* your ability, and a time when lack of confidence caused you to *underestimate* your ability. What happened? How would you approach those situations now? How could you stem excessive pride or boost your self-confidence?
- Do Activity 3 in pairs.
- Create a class collage with the theme "How We Show Humility" (Question 4 of "What I Think"). This might be done by having each student make a small individual collage and then combining them, or by making a large group collage.

Wrapping It Up: (5–10 minutes)

Give each student a chance to share what most surprised them about the *anavah* unit and how they plan to have more *anavah* in their lives.

Home–School Connection

Students should go home and share with their parents how they are going to increase *anavah* in their lives.

Conclusion

Over the course of the year we have been engaging in the mitzvah of *Talmud Torah* (study of Torah) as it relates to Jewish values and the self.

We have explored *k'vod habriyot* (individual dignity). We looked at *k'vod habriyot* in the classroom, drew inspiration from Rose Schneiderman who championed the dignity of workers, and examined other champions of dignity.

We talked about *t'shuvah* as repentance and talked about *t'shuvah* as returning to our better selves. We celebrated Rosh Hashanah and used the sound of the shofar to help us both with repenting and with returning to our better selves. We looked at Beit T'shuvah and the phenomenal work it has done in helping people turn their lives around. We thought about what we want to change in our own lives.

We read about *sameach b'chelko* (personal satisfaction). We sat in our sukkah and contemplated how we enjoy and appreciate what we have. We wrote a poem, song, or rap about the ideas of *sameach b'chelko.*

Finally we considered the value of *anavah* (humility). We listened to the Muppets sing about how hard it is to be humble when you are perfect in every way. This is one of the harder values to incorporate in our American lifestyle because it is not one that particularly overlaps with contemporary American values.

We hope that we have grown—as a class and as individuals—over the course of our learning Jewish values. We are ready now to turn from the examination of values relating to the self to values relating to the family.

PART 2
Lesson Plans for Volume 2: Family Connections

LESSON PLANS FOR VOLUME 2: FAMILY CONNECTIONS

Introduction

Volume 2 of the *Living Jewish Values* series expands from the individual to the family. The family is the first community to which we belong, and the lessons and values we learn from our families influence how we live in the future. In this volume we find the values of:

- *Hakarat Hatov* (Gratitude)
- *Sh'lom Bayit* (Family Harmony)
- *Emet* (Truth)
- *Kedushah* (Holiness)

The value of *hakarat hatov* (gratitude) is further enhanced in the holiday lesson for Chanukah, and the value of *kedushah* (holiness) is further explored in the holiday lesson for Shavuot.

While many of the features of the first volume carry over into the second volume, you will notice that the format of the second volume is a little different. The "time capsule" activity has been replaced with a "concept map," ideal for a visual conception of the value at hand. Students, teachers, and families will find these concept maps very helpful, and they have been incorporated into most of the chapter plans.

ESSENTIAL QUESTIONS

	LESSON 1	LESSON 2	LESSON 3
CHAPTER 1 *Hakarat Hatov* Gratitude	How do we demonstrate *hakarat hatov* for friends and strangers?	How do we demonstrate *hakarat hatov* for our families?	How do we demonstrate *hakarat hatov* for God?
CHAPTER 2 *Sh'lom Bayit* Family harmony	What is *sh'lom bayit?*	How important is *sh'lom bayit?*	What risks can we take for the sake of *sh'lom bayit?*
CHAPTER 3 *Emet* Truth	Why is truth so important?	How much is truth worth?	How is truth important?
CHAPTER 4 *Kedushah* Holiness	What does it mean to find holiness in time, in space, and between people?	How can I expand my *kedushah* range?	What about God?

VOLUME 2 • CHAPTER 1

Hakarat Hatov, Lesson 1 of 3

Essential Question: How do we demonstrate hakarat hatov *(gratitude) for friends and strangers?*

Lesson Objectives: Students will be able to:

1 Define *hakarat hatov.*

2 Articulate reasons for *hakarat hatov.*

3. Demonstrate appreciation for friends.

4. Plan ways to express appreciation for the things that strangers do for us.

Getting Started: (10–15 minutes)

POSTER BOARD QUESTION. What is something in your life for which you are grateful?

- Seat the students in a circle in the classroom, either at their desks or on the floor. Students take turns going around the room and saying something nice about their classmates one by one. (Very large classes may choose to do this in more than one circle.) A faster alternative would be to have each child say something nice about the student sitting next to him/her, instead of about everyone.

Exploring the Text: (15 minutes)

- As a class, read the opening, introduction, and "Cultivate Gratitude" sidebar.
- Discuss: What is *hakarat hatov*? Why is it a Jewish value?
- In pairs, read the *Hakarat Hatov* Superstar.

Experiential Learning: (5 minutes)

- Have students work on Activity 1 about the family lens.

Wrapping It Up: (5–10 minutes)

Sit in a circle again. Go around, each student telling how he/she is going to show appreciation to a stranger (i.e., say thank-you to the bagger at the supermarket) and how he/she is going to show appreciation to a friend.

Home–School Connection

Ask students to complete the personality quiz at home.

VOLUME 2 • CHAPTER 1

Hakarat Hatov, Lesson 2 of 3

Essential Question: How do we demonstrate hakarat hatov for our families?

Lesson Objectives: Students will be able to:

1. Articulate areas of gratitude to parents, siblings, grandparents.
2. Demonstrate appreciation for their families.

Getting Started: (5–10 minutes)

POSTER BOARD QUESTION: When was a time when someone thanked you or expressed appreciation for something that you did?

- Ask the class: Why do we have Mother's Day? What is it for? Why do we have Father's Day? What is it for? Does it do what it is supposed to do? Is it a good thing or a bad thing that we have one special day a year to celebrate mothers and fathers? What is the value we are studying called and what does it mean?

Exploring the Text: (3–5 minutes)

Have students silently reread the first page of the chapter to refresh their memories.

Experiential Learning: (25–30 minutes)

- Make a class list of things that siblings have done for the students in the class and how the students plan to show appreciation to their siblings.
- Individual work: Write a poem of appreciation to a family member. It can be a parent, a grandparent, a sibling, an aunt or uncle, etc. Copy the poem on a clean piece of paper and illustrate it.
- As students finish their illustrated poems, direct them to do Activity 1 about the family lens.
- In pairs, work on "What I Think," questions 1–3. Each student writes his/her own answers, but they work together and help each other think of and enrich their examples.

Wrapping It Up: (5 minutes)

Those who wish share their poems. Post all poems on the bulletin board for a week or two, then take them down and have students give them to the people they are about.

Home–School Connection

Ask students to work on Activity 3, the two-week gratitude chart.

VOLUME 2 • CHAPTER 1

Hakarat Hatov, Lesson 3 of 3

Essential Question: How do we demonstrate hakarat hatov *for God?*

Lesson Objectives: Students will be able to:

1. List areas where we should be grateful to God.
2. Recite Birkat Hagomel.

Getting Started: (3–5 minutes)

POSTER BOARD QUESTION: What is one thing in the natural world that you really like?

- Play the Hebrew song: "Todah al Kol Mah Shebarata," which can be found at www.youtube.com/watch?v=w2_IhVecx3Q. For the English translation, go to www.hebrewsongs.com/song-toda.htm.

Exploring the Text: (5–10 minutes)

- Dramatic reading of the Agaddic tradition of Leah naming her son Yehudah.
- Read as a class the first paragraph of Hakarat Hatov in History.

Experiential Learning: (20–30 minutes)

- Divide the class into three groups. One group studies the bikkurim offering section, the second learns about Birkat Hagomel and the third does the Lea Goldberg poem. Some teachers may decide to substitute the Todah al Kol mah Shebarata poem instead, or to add this poem as a 4th group if it is a really big class.
- Each group reads its assigned part, answers the questions, and prepares a presentation to the whole group so everyone can benefit from what they learned.
- Have the class come back together and each group present what it learned and teaches it to the rest of the class.

Wrapping It Up: (5–10 minutes)

Everyone practices Birkat Hagomel and if time allows, those who choose share an experience when they did or could have done Birkat Hagomel.

Home–School Connection

Have students continue doing Activity 3, the two-week gratitude chart.

VOLUME 2 • CHAPTER 2

Sh'lom Bayit, Lesson 1 of 3

Essential Question: What is sh'lom bayit?

Note to teachers: When teaching *sh'lom bayit,* great care must be taken to distinguish between the importance of working together to create family harmony and putting up with abuse for the sake of "family harmony." We also must be sensitive to real-life family issues. There will be children in the classroom whose perfectly happily married parents had a fight last night, and children in the classroom whose parents are divorced and fighting acrimoniously in court. The classroom should not become a platform for children to share private family matters with the class, nor should children learn that putting up with abuse at home is a Jewish value called *sh'lom bayit*.

Lesson Objectives: Students will be able to:

1. Translate the word *sh'lom.*
2. Translate the word *bayit.*
3. Define *sh'lom bayit* in terms of siblings and family togetherness.

Getting Started: (10–15 minutes)

POSTER BOARD QUESTION: What is the difference between a house and a home?

- What does *bayit* mean? *(house or home)*
- What does *sh'lom* mean? *(hello, goodbye, peace)* Why do you think we use the word "peace" as a greeting and a parting? What does that tell us about peace?
- Draw a picture of what you think *sh'lom bayit* might look like. Share the pictures. What is the class idea of what *sh'lom bayit* is? Judaism teaches that *sh'lom bayit* is peace within the house, or family harmony.

Exploring the Text: (10–15 minutes)

- Rabbi Yisrael Meir Kagen, known as the Chofetz Chaim, was a rabbi in the late 1800s and early 1900s. His focus was on how people should speak to each other and about each other. Read the Agaddic tradition story of the Chofetz Chaim together on page16. What do you think is the next thing that might happen in the story? What might Jacob say or do? What might the parents say or do? What might Sarah say or do?
- Ask students to do Activity 2 individually or in pairs.

Experiential Learning: (5–10 minutes)

Have students work individually on "What I Think," question 1. Students can write a story, a dialogue, a play, or a poem.

Wrapping It Up: (5–10 minutes)

A rabbinic legend: There are two angels who visit on Friday nights, a good angel and a bad angel. When they get to the house, they look to see what is happening. If the candles are lit, if the children helped get the house ready, if the family members are spending time together, then the good angel smiles and says: "May it be like this every week. This is *sh'lom bayit.*"

Home–School Connection

Have students complete "What I Think," question 3 at home.

VOLUME 2 • CHAPTER 2

Sh'lom Bayit, Lesson 2 of 3

Essential Question: How important is sh'lom bayit?

Lesson Objectives: Students will be able to:

1. Expand the definition of *sh'lom bayit* to include the parents in the family.
2. Have a sense of the importance of *sh'lom bayit*.
3. Begin to think about prioritizing values: *sh'lom bayit* over strict truth; safety over *sh'lom bayit.*

Getting Started: (3–5 minutes)

POSTER BOARD QUESTION. What activity (or activities) does your family enjoy doing together?

- Review: What is *sh'lom bayit*?

Exploring the Text I: (10–15 minutes)

- Have students read the sidebar "God Tells a White Lie," story only.
- Have three students act out the story.
- Discuss: Why did God change what Sarah said? Was God right to change what Sarah said? Examine further the idea that God did not want Abraham and Sarah to have any reason to be mad at each other or to be hurt by what was said.
- Read the rest of the sidebar.

Experiential Learning: (15 minutes)

- Have students complete Activity 1 about active listening individually. Then, in pairs, have them practice some of the active listening skills listed in this activity.
- Ask students to do Activity 3 individually.

Exploring the Text II: (10–15 minutes)

- Read the Rabbi Meir story that opens this chapter. Discuss:
  - What do you think this story is trying to teach? *(that the relationship between husbands and wives is even more important than the rabbi's dignity)*
  - Do you like the story? Which character(s) in the story do you like? Which character(s) in the story do you not like?
  - Rabbi Meir was trying to help his student out by giving her a way to spit in his face so that her husband would take her back. Can you think of other ways Rabbi Meir might have helped this student and her husband improve the *sh'lom bayit* in their home? Can you think of ways Rabbi Meir might have helped this student, but not increased *sh'lom bayit* in her home?

Wrapping It Up: (5 minutes)

In this same chapter we learned that the value of *sh'lom bayit* is so important that God shaded the truth to promote *sh'lom bayit* between Abraham and Sarah. Can you think of values or situations where something is more important than *sh'lom bayit*? Do you think this might have been one of them?

Home–School Connection

Have students complete the "How do you face the heat?" personality quiz.

VOLUME 2 • CHAPTER 2

Sh'lom Bayit, Lesson 3 of 3

Essential Question: What risks can we take for the sake of sh'lom bayit?

Lesson Objectives: Students will be able to:

1. Apply the concept of *sh'lom bayit* to familiar Torah stories.
2. Use the Judah and Joseph story as an example of risk-taking for the sake of *sh'lom bayit.*
3. Consider ways to incorporate *sh'lom bayit* in their own lives.

Getting Started: (5–10 minutes)

POSTER BOARD QUESTION: Who is your favorite aunt or uncle and why?

- Make a list on the board of family pairs: husbands and wives; parents and children; brothers and sisters.

Exploring the Text: (3–5 minutes)

- Read together as a class Judah's emotional plea to his brother in the orange box on page 16. Read it through without discussion.

Experiential Learning: (30 minutes)

- Red. Have students underline the word "father" every time it appears. How many times does it appear? Write the number next to the red oval. Discuss briefly: Why does Judah use the word "father" so many times?
- In advance, prepare index cards with the assignments for each group. That way, once you divide the class into groups and hand out the assignments, you can move around the room to help out as needed.
- Divide the class into three small groups. Each group will explore one of the three boxes and then will share with the class as a whole. (If it is a large class, divide into six groups and assign two groups to each box.)
- Blue. *Vayigash Yehudah* (Judah drew near). Read the blue box about Judah drawing near to the man that he does not yet know is his brother Joseph. Do you agree that Judah took emotional risks in drawing close? As a group, draw a picture, write a poem, or plan a skit to show how you might become close to your own family.
- Green. Read the green box together as a group. Each student should think of an answer to the question at the bottom of the box. They do not have to share the answer with their classmates—it might be private. As a group, invent a fictitious answer to the question and draw a picture, write a poem, or plan a skit to show a painful family reality.
- Pink. Read the pink box together as a group. Then open a *Chumash* and read the rest of the chapter together. How does Joseph show empathy to his brothers? How can empathy build *sh'lom bayit* in your house? As a group, draw a picture, write a poem, or plan a skit showing how empathy can help build *sh'lom bayit.*
- Have groups present their pictures, poems, and skits to the class.

Wrapping It Up: (5–10 minutes)
Reflect as a class on ways that *sh'lom bayit* can be a reality in our own lives.

Home–School Connection
Ask the students to complete the *Sh'lom Bayit* Superstar, and have them share the fictitious interview with thier parents and have a discussion about the issues it raises.

VOLUME 2 • CHAPTER 3

Emet, Lesson 1 of 3

Essential Question: Why is truth so important?

Lesson Objectives: Students will be able to:

1. Articulate how society is based on trust and honesty.
2. Differentiate between self-serving lies and lies that the tradition sees as valid to the smooth running of society.

Getting Started: (5 minutes)

POSTER BOARD QUESTION: It says in Psalms: "Who may dwell in God's tent? They who live without blame, who do what is right, and who acknowledge the truth in their heart." What do you think that means?

- Review from Chapter 2: Have students act out the story of how God misreported Sarah's words to Abraham in the interests of *sh'lom bayit*.

Exploring the Text: (10–15 minutes)

- Read the opening story about Rav, his wife, and their son, Hiyya.
- Discuss: What is the difference between this story and the story of God lying to Abraham? Both are about keeping the peace between husband and wife. Why is the message in one that it is okay to lie, but in the other that despite good intentions, it is not okay to lie?
- Read aloud the paragraph beginning: "All relationships require trust . . ."

Experiential Learning: (25–35 minutes)

- Have students work in pairs on Activity 1 on page 24. This is an exercise about telling the truth and accepting the consequences.
- Study the concept map on page 26 together as a class.
- Discuss: Do you agree with the idea that society rests on honesty? Do you agree that there are times when honesty is not the best policy? Do you agree with the examples given here for times when it is okay to shade the truth some?
- Dramatic representation. Divide the students into groups of three and ask them to develop a short skit. Skits might demonstrate a situation where it is not clear whether it is better to tell the truth or to tell a white lie; or, they might demonstrate a time when people lie for self-serving reasons. After each group presents its skit to the class, there should be a short discussion about the choice.

Wrapping It Up: (5 minutes)

Read together: "Truth: A Foundation For All Relationships" on page 22.

Home–School Connection

Ask students to watch with their parents the You Tube video www.youtube.com/watch?v=Jexx00EkXKE&feature=fvsr about the family that might forgo a $50,000 win on the grounds that it is better to be honest. Do you think the insurance company should pay? Do you think the parents are teaching their sons the right lesson?

VOLUME 2 • CHAPTER 3

Emet, Lesson 2 of 3

Essential Question: How much is truth worth?

Lesson Objectives: Students will be able to:

1. Consider honesty in a larger social framework.
2. Think about honesty in sports competitions.
3. Think about honesty and fairness in the courtroom.
4. Think about honesty regarding handling of property.

Getting Started: (10 minutes)

POSTER BOARD QUESTION: The prophet Zechariah said: "These are the things you must do: Speak truth to one another, and render true and perfect justice." How do you do that in your life?

- Summarize the story of the twins and the hockey shot that the students were assigned to do at home. Ask for the students' and their families' reactions from their discussion. Did they think the family in the story handled this correctly? Was a mistake made? If so, what was it? Does the boy deserve the $50,000 for making the shot? If you were the sponsor of the contest, would you pay the $50,000? Focus on the fact that the father allowed his son to lie in the first place by letting the wrong boy take the shot. The danger of lying is that you get caught in your lie and have to continue making up more lies to cover up the previous ones. This father refused to get stuck. He admitted his mistake and decided not to continue in the charade.

Exploring the Text: (10 minutes)

Agaddic Tradition. In pairs, have the students read the story and complete Activity 2.

Experiential Learning: (15 minutes)

***EMET* SUPERSTAR**

- Have the students read the *Emet* Superstar silently (or read aloud as a class, if you prefer) .
- Ask: Who is the *Emet* Superstar in this chapter? Is it Jimmy Bain? The child who did what he thought he was supposed to do? What about Barry Scheck and Peter Neufeld?
- Have a mini-debate, with different students supporting different "superstars."

Wrapping It Up: (5 minutes)

Ask students to reflect on the question: How much is truth worth?

Home–School Connection

Complete the "What flavor are you" personality quiz? Share at home.

VOLUME 2 • CHAPTER 3

Emet, Lesson 3 of 3

Essential Question: How important is truth?

Note to teachers: You may not have sufficient time for both of the experiential learning projects given here. If that's the case, then choose which one fits your class better and do that one. You can always have the students do the other activity individually in their books.

Lesson Objectives: Students will be able to:

1. Think about related issues, such as exaggeration and tattling.
2. Relate to truth metaphorically.
3. Discuss how their vision of truth has changed after doing this chapter.

Getting Started:

POSTER BOARD QUESTION: We all know the story of George Washington and the cherry tree. When did you tell the truth in a difficult situation?

- Play a song about honesty for the students. One suggestion is "Honesty" by Billy Joel. Audio only would probably be best for this, but if using You Tube, be careful to screen the clip in advance for inappropriate ads, sidebar pictures, etc.

Experiential Learning I: (30 minutes)

- Designate a corner of the room for each of the four questions in the "What I Think" section. Let students choose which question they want to work on. Have each group work on the question and come up with a good answer and a helpful presentation. Presentations should include both the question and the answer. Give time after each presentation for questions and comments from the rest of the class.

Experiential Learning II: (20 minutes)

- Have students do Activity 3 individually. Then divide into pairs, compare answers, and combine imagery. When each pair has one good answer for each of the three items, mix the pairs up and do it again. When the class has narrowed its imagery down to two or three items for each one, come back together as a class and share responses.

Wrapping It Up: (5 minutes)
Ask the students: How has what we studied in this chapter changed how you think about truth in your life?

VOLUME 2 • CHAPTER 4

Kedushah, Lesson 1 of 3

Essential Question: What does it mean to find holiness in time, in space, and between people?

Lesson Objectives: Students will be able to:

1. Explain holiness in time.
2. Explain holiness in space.
3. Explain holiness between people.

Getting Started: (10 minutes)

POSTER BOARD QUESTION: When I hear the word "holiness" I think of . . .

- Begin with the Kedushah prayer. (For the purposes of this introduction, it does not matter which Kedushah you use —weekday, Shabbat morning, Shabbat Musaf, etc.—) If your class has already learned the Kedushah, have them open the siddur and sing it. If they have not learned it yet, have it sung to them (you, the cantor, a student in a higher class, a tape). Ask them to count how many times the root word *kadosh* shows up in the prayer. No wonder it is called the *kedushah*!

Exploring the Text: (5 minutes)

Have the students take the "Where do you find holiness?" quiz on page 35. Divide the students into groups according to their results: green (time trackin'); blue (people person); red (a place for everything)

Experiential Learning: (30 minutes)

- Blue group: As a group, discuss who lifts your spirit and helps you find holiness. Is it your parent? Your teacher? Your rabbi? Prepare a presentation for the class about how people add to the holiness in your life and how you might incorporate the lessons you are learning to bring holiness to other people.
- Green group: As a group, discuss what time feels most holy to you. Is it a particular time of day? Shabbat? A specific holiday? Prepare a presentation for the class about why time brings holiness to your life and how you can share those times with other people.
- Red group: As a group, discuss what place feels most holy to you. Is it outside in nature? In the synagogue? When you are surrounded by special things? Prepare a presentation for the class about holy space and how you can share your holy spaces with other people.
- Have the groups present to the rest of the class.
- Discuss: What views of holiness came out of the presentations? Did any group convince you to change your mind about where you find holiness?

Wrapping It Up

Discuss: What is the difference between finding holiness in time, in space, or between people? Are those the only choices? What else might be holy? *(God, Torah, mitzvot, studying/learning/knowledge, fine art, music)*

Home–School Connection

Have a discussion at home about where holiness is found. Where do your parents find holiness? Is it the same place you find holiness?

VOLUME 2 • CHAPTER 4

Kedushah, Lesson 2 of 3

Essential Question: How can I expand my kedushah *range?*

Lesson Objectives: Students will be able to:

1. Explore *kedushah* (holiness) through different avenues.
2. Understand the relationship between *kedushah* (holiness) and the Kiddush.
3. Enjoy the variety of ways to achieve *kedushah* (holiness).

Getting Started: (5 minutes)

POSTER BOARD QUESTION: Who do you know who acts in a holy way?

- Ask: What is the Friday night prayer with the wine/grape juice called? (*Kiddush*). Note that this is the same word as *kedushah*. Tell them to count the times the word *kadosh* shows up in this section of the Kiddush. (*6*)
- Play www.youtube.com/watch?v=r41BCIkyGsc. What is being sanctified/made holy? (*Shabbat*)

Exploring the Text / Experiential Learning: (30–40 minutes)

During the last lesson, students self-identified as people who are more likely to find holiness in time (green group), in space (red group), or between people (blue group) and worked on their own chosen kind of holiness. In this lesson, students will explore the other ways holiness can be found.

FOCUS ON *HOLINESS IN SPACE* FOR THE GREEN AND BLUE GROUPS:

- Read about the Israeli poet Rachel in *Kedushah* Superstar, page 37.
- Read, discuss, and draw a mural of one of her poems: el artzi / to my country, found at www.poetryinternational.org/piw_cms/cms/cms_module/index.php?obj_id=3271
- Where did Rachel find holiness? Can you feel some of the holiness of the land of Israel and particularly of the kinneret region of Israel coming through in her poem?
- Has anyone in the group been to Israel? Did you feel holiness there?
- You are someone who is more likely to find holiness in time or holiness between people than holiness in space. Nonetheless, where (what place) do you find holiness?

FOCUS ON *HOLINESS IN TIME* FOR THE BLUE AND RED GROUPS:

- You looked at the Friday night Kiddush at the beginning of the lesson. Compare this version to the one recited on a festival evening. How many times does the word *kadosh* show up in the paragraph following *borei p'ri hagafen*? (*5*) What is being sanctified/made holy in the final blessing in this Kiddush? *(the people of Israel and the festivals)*
- Each group member draw a picture of when you might find *kedushah*/holiness. Is it on Shabbat? On a particular holiday? If so, which one? At a particular time of day? Put the drawings together and create a group collage.
- Look at the different examples of holiness-in-time that your group came up with. What do they have in common? What are differences between them?
- You are a person who is more likely to find holiness between people or holiness in space. Nonetheless, when do you feel more holy?

Continued on next page

VOLUME 2 • CHAPTER 4

Kedushah, Lesson 2 of 3, Continued

FOCUS ON *HOLINESS BETWEEN PEOPLE* FOR THE GREEN AND RED GROUPS:

- Read the Agaddic tradition on page 36
- Discuss: "If loving-kindness toward birds and beasts can save the world, how much more so can loving-kindness practiced toward other human beings, who are created in the image of God." What acts of loving-kindness have you experienced or heard about that helped bring holiness into the world?
- Each group member draw a picture of an act of loving-kindness that helps to bring holiness into the world. Put the pictures together and make a collage, or create a group mural with the drawings.
- Look at the different examples of holiness-producing acts that your group came up with. What do they have in common? What are differences between them?
- You are a person who usually finds holiness in time or in space. Nonetheless, how do these acts help make you a better Jew?

Wrapping It Up: (10 minutes)
Make a display of the different group murals in the classroom or along the hallway. Reflect on all the different ways your class has identified to find and bring *kedushah* (holiness) into the world.

Home–School connection:
Explore the *kedushah* concept map with your parents.

VOLUME 2 • CHAPTER 4

Kedushah, Lesson 3 of 3

Essential Question: What about God?

Lesson Objectives: Students will be able to:

1. Relate to holiness as *imitatio Dei*—imitating God, being like God. As God is holy, so must the people of Israel be holy.
2. See holiness as part of God's relationship with the Jewish people as a community.
3. Be aware of the connection between God taking the people of Israel out of Egypt and the requirement of the people of Israel to be holy.
4. Understand that the mandate to be holy includes all walks of life, including ethical and ritual.

Getting Started: (5 minutes)

POSTER BOARD QUESTION: What is one holy thing you have done in your life?

- Play the song "Kedoshim Tihiyu," found at http://youtu.be/xLFXIaeJVb0.

Exploring the Text: (15–20 minutes)

- Read together from the *Chumash* Leviticus 19:2. *"Kedoshim tihiyu, ki kadosh ani."* ("You shall be holy, for I, the Lord your God, am holy.")
- Discuss: Why do you think the command is in the second person **plural** (*tihiyu*)? (*possible interpretations: to teach that it is not a command for exceptional people, but that it is a command for all of us; to teach that holiness is found from being part of communities rather than by going off alone for a spiritual experience)*
- This is Parashat Kedoshim, the *parashah* that talks about how to be holy. What sorts of things are part of being holy? Some examples you might point out in the chapter: sacrifices, verses 5–8; leaving food in the field for the poor, verses 9–10; honesty, verses 11–13, 15–16, 35–36; not putting a stumbling block before the blind, verse 14; not eating blood, verse 26; respect for the elderly, verse 32; treating the stranger well, verses 33–34. *[Note: Parashat Kedoshim (chapter 20) also deals with laws of sexual relationships. If any student raises the issue, just say that appropriate sexual behavior is part of holiness too, and leave it at that. If you have a particularly persistent student, tell him/her that this is not the appropriate time or place to explore that issue and move on.]*
- Be sure to point out the connection between God taking the people of Israel out of Egypt and the requirement of the people of Israel to be holy.

Experiential Learning: (15–20 minutes)

- See the story of God's sparks of holiness on page 32.
- Individual work. Use your creativity. Choose one of the following ideas or create your own. Write a letter to God, telling God about your quest to find the missing sparks. Design a treasure hunt for classmates or younger students giving clues where they might find the sparks and what they have to do to pick up those sparks. Make a board game teaching about ways to "pick up" sparks of holiness. Write a story about someone who found sparks and what that person did with them.

Wrapping It Up

Give a summary of the *kedushah* chapter, including relating to God and finding holiness in time, in space, and between people.

Conclusion

Congratulations! You and your class have now completed the second volume of the *Living Jewish Values* series, Family Connections.

You talked about how to demonstrate *hakarat hatov* (gratitude) for strangers, for friends and family, and for God. Your students worked to actualize *hakarat hatov* in their own lives and learned strategies to increase their appreciation of others. Chanukah came and gave the students an opportunity to "do" *hakarat hatov* each night, showing appreciation to or of different people.

You talked about *sh'lom bayit* (family harmony) as a core Jewish value, and examined what to do when it conflicts with other values, such as strict honesty.

Appropriately, you went from *sh'lom bayit* straight into an examination of the critical importance of honesty in the world and in the Jewish tradition.

And you concluded the year with an exploration of *kedushah* (holiness), including the *kedushah* of Torah study on Shavuot.

Yashar ko'ach and *ken yirbu*! May your opportunities for learning and teaching increase.

PART 3
Lesson Plans for Jewish Holidays

INTRODUCTION

Sounding the shofar on Rosh Hashanah to help us reach our better selves … sitting in the sukkah enjoying our bounty … appreciating miracles on Chanukah … feeding the hungry at Purim … being a good guest and a good host at Pesach … immersing ourselves in the *kedushah* of Torah on Shavuot—there are few better times for inculcating Jewish values than during holidays. This lesson plan manual includes a lesson for each of the major holidays throughout the school year: Rosh Hashanah/Yom Kippur, Sukkot, Chanukah, Purim, Pesach, and Shavuot. Four of these holidays reinforce values taught in the *Living Jewish Values* series volumes I and II, and two of the holidays teach specific values not addressed in those volumes. Holidays are celebrated in school, at home, and in the synagogue. The lessons offered here will help the students realize the values already within the holiday observances.

ESSENTIAL QUESTIONS

HOLIDAY	VALUE	ESSENTIAL QUESTION
ROSH HASHANAH AND YOM KIPPUR	*T'shuvah* Returning to Your Best Self	How does the sound of the shofar help us to do *t'shuvah*?
SUKKOT	*Sameach B'chelko* Personal Satisfaction	How do we show that we are happy with what we have on Sukkot?
CHANUKAH	*Hakarat Hatov* Gratitude	How can we enhance the *hakarat hatov* aspects of Chanukah?
PURIM	*Ma'achil R'eivim* Feeding the Hungry	How does Purim teach us about the year-round obligation to feed the hungry?
PESACH	*Hakhnasat Orchim* Hospitality	How can I fulfill the mitzvah of *hakhnasat orchim* at the seder by being a good guest or a good host?
SHAVUOT	*Kedushah* Holiness	How do we demonstrate the *kedushah* of Torah?

Rosh Hashanah and Yom Kippur: T'shuvah

Essential Question: How does the sound of the shofar help us do t'shuvah?

Teacher's Note: This lesson assumes that the students have already done the "What does t'shuvah mean" lesson, *Living Jewish Values Volume I*, Chapter 2, Lesson 1.

Lesson Objectives: Students will be able to:

1. Recognize and explain the machzor's position that: "*U't'shuvah, u't'filah, u'tzedakah ma'avirin et ro'ah hagezerah*; namely, that returning to one's best self, prayer, and seeking justice can change the severity of the judgment."
2. Apply what they previously learned about *t'shuvah* to the holidays of Rosh Hashanah and Yom Kippur.
3. Hear the shofar and feel a stirring to come back to one's best self.

Getting Started: (3 minutes)
Begin the class with proper shofar blasts.

Exploring the Text: (5 minutes)
The machzor says: "returning to one's best self, prayer, and seeking justice can change the severity of the judgment." This does not mean that if we all pray really hard and give tzedakah, everything will be perfect in our lives. The real world does not work that way. But it does mean that seeking our better selves *(t'shuvah)*, joining with the community in prayer *(t'filah)*, and seeking justice in the world *(tzedakah)* can make our lives different. Those things can make it easier to handle difficult times, when they happen.

Experiential Learning: (20–25 minutes)

- In pairs, ask each other the following questions:
    - How do you think *t'shuvah, t'filah* and *tzedakah* can make it easier to handle the difficult times?
    - Specifically *t'shuvah* —how can *t'shuvah* make your life different?
    - How do you feel when you hear the shofar?
- Join together as a class and have each person tell the class how his/her partner answered the questions.
- Ask the class: Why do you think we need ten days of repentance (two days of Rosh Hashanah, a week in between, and Yom Kippur) to deal with *t'shuvah*? Do we really need so much time? And why do you think Rosh Hashanah and Yom Kippur are a week apart instead of having them at different times of the year?
- Ask the class: What is the point of sounding the shofar? Do you think it works? Note that the shofar is sounded at morning services for the entire month of Elul and on Rosh Hashanah (except Shabbat). (The shofar blast when Yom Kippur is over is qualitatively different.)
- Have each student write a private meditation to bring to the synagogue to say right before or during the sounding of the shofar.

Wrapping It Up: (10 minutes)
Give each student a chance to sound the shofar.

Sukkot: Sameach B'chelko

Essential Question: How do we show that we are happy with what we have on Sukkot?

Teacher's Note: This lesson does not assume that children have been introduced to the idea of *sameach b'chelko.*

Lesson Objectives: Students will be able to:

1. Define *sameach b'chelko.*
2. Apply the value to the holiday of Sukkot.

Getting Started: (15 minutes)

- Ask the class to draw pictures, individually, of the safest place they can imagine. Give 5 minutes for drawing and another 5 minutes for sharing. Pictures will probably show fortresses, walls, locks and keys, etc.
- Ask the class: Which is safer: a very well-locked and alarmed house in a high-risk neighborhood, or an unlocked house in a quiet place where everyone is honest?
- Can we lock up our sukkah? What do we learn from that?

Exploring the Text: (5–7 minutes)

- In small groups or as a class, read the verses about Sukkot from Parashat Re'eh and answer the questions below.
  "After you have harvested grain and fruit, you shall hold the Feast of Booths for seven days. You shall rejoice in your festival with your son and daughter, your servants, the Levites, the stranger, and orphan and the widow in your communities" (Deut. 16:13–14).
  - Who celebrates Sukkot? *(everyone)*
  - When is Sukkot? *(according to this, after the harvest. Other places in the Torah tell that it begins on the 15th day of the 7th month, which is Tishre.)*
  - What American holiday is based on the idea of celebrating when the harvest is in? *(Thanksgiving—the Pilgrims knew the Bible well!)*
  - What are we commanded to do on Sukkot? *(rejoice)*

Experiential Learning: (15–20 minutes)

- Class discussion: We are commanded to rejoice, or be happy on Sukkot. What are we supposed to be happy about? (*The harvest, in other words, we are supposed to be happy with what we produce, happy with what we have. That is called* sameach b'chelko.) How do we show that we are happy with what we have on Sukkot? (*We decorate the sukkah with signs of the harvest; we sit in an unlocked, unalarmed sukkah; we invite guests over to share with us; we sing songs)*
- Pirkei Avot says: Who is rich? The person who is happy with what s/he has. Make this saying into a sukkah decoration to bring home or to hang in the school sukkah.

Wrapping It Up

In some places people sit in the sukkah in the snow and eat their soup with mittens on. In other places people bring portable air conditioners into their sukkot. What is it like where you live? Share some weather-related Sukkot stories.

Chanukah: Hakarat Hatov

Essential Question: How can we enhance the hakarat hatov aspects of Chanukah?

Lesson Objectives: Students will be able to:

1. Appreciate the Maccabees for persevering and not giving up.
2. Reflect on the meaning of the *Al Hanisim* prayer.
3. Demonstrate *hakarat hatov* each night of Chanukah.

Getting Started: (5–10 minutes)

- Read the following bibliodrama to the class:

  You are among the Maccabees and have been fighting the Assyrian Greeks for several years. Now they have left Jerusalem and the Temple is in Jewish hands again! You are weary and tired; but, along with everyone else, you are very excited. It seems like it has been so long since Jews were allowed in the Temple. You can't wait to go in. You were only there once before when you were a child, and you remember how gorgeous it was! But when you enter the Temple area, you cannot believe your eyes. You look around and see piles of garbage. Those bones over there—the ones the dog is sniffing—you are sure those are pig bones. Everyone gets very quiet. The Temple is a mess. It is dirty and it smells. There is a big idol of the king right in the middle of the courtyard. The *ner tamid* (eternal light) is not burning and there is no olive oil to be seen.

- Ask the students: What do you say and/or do at this moment? Give as many students as possible a chance to say what they would do. Suggest that they answer in the first person, and even encourage them to have discussions with each other.

Experiential Learning (35 minutes)

- Discussion: (5 minutes) Why do we display Chanukah candles in the window? *(so that everyone can see the candles, to publicize the miracle, to show that we appreciate miracles in the world, to spread the light)*
- Text study, in pairs: (10 minutes)
  - Open a siddur to the *Al Hanisim* prayer. During what holidays is this prayer said? *(Chanukah, Purim, and in some communities, Yom Ha'atzma'ut)*
  - Where in the siddur is it found? *(in the* Amidah *and the* Birkat Hamazon*)*
  - What does *Al Hanisim* mean? *(for the [following] miracles [O Lord, we thank You])*
  - In your pairs, read the prayer.
  - What surprises you about *Al Hanisim* ? *(no mention of the oil burning for eight days, no mention of the Maccabees, unusually strong emphasis on God)*
  - What is the point of the prayer? *(to thank God for the miracles, to remind us not to take things for granted, to make us think about miracles in our time and what they might look like)*
  - Not taking things for granted and expressing appreciation is called *hakarat hatov.*

Continued on next page

Chanukah: Hakarat Hatov, Continued

- Writing project: (20 minutes) Ask the students to write a meditation for each night of Chanukah, expressing gratitude and appreciation for something different each night:
  - 1st night—something God has done for the Jewish community.
  - 2nd night—something God has done for your family.
  - 3rd night—something God has done for you personally.
  - 4th night—something your grandparents have done for you.
  - 5th night—something your parents have done for you.
  - 6th night—something a stranger has done for you.
  - 7th night—something each of your siblings has done for you.
  - 8th night—something God has done for the world.

Wrapping It Up: (5 minutes)
Give students a chance to share one of their meditations. Encourage students to read their meditations at home when they light the Chanukah candles with their families.

Purim: Ma'achil R'eivim

Essential Question: How does Purim teach us about the year-round obligation to feed the hungry?

Lesson Objectives: Students will be able to:

1. Define the mitzvah of *mishlo'ach manot.*
2. Define the mitzvah of *matanot la'evyonim.*
3. Study Yad Chessed as a model of *ma'achil r'eivim.*

Getting Started: (5–10 minutes)

PUZZLE GAME

Teacher prepares in advance index cards with the verse that follows (adapted from Esther 9:22), one word or phrase written on each card (as shown). Have students, either as a class or in smaller groups, lay out the cards so that the words appear in order and make sense.

The Jews | were to observe | the fourteenth | day | of Adar | as a | day of | feasting and | merrymaking | and as an | occasion for | sending | gifts | to one another | and presents | to the poor

Experiential Learning

DEBRIEFING THE PUZZLE GAME (5–10 minutes)

- What is the 14th of Adar? *(Purim)*
- According to this verse, what are Jews supposed to do on Purim? *(send gifts to one another and give presents to the poor)*
- What do most of us do on Purim? *(answers may include: dress up, hear the megillah, make noise when Haman's name is read, eat hamantashen)* Explain that we are also supposed to send gifts to one another and give presents to the poor.
    - Send gifts to one another—this is called *mishlo'ach manot*— "Purim baskets" of food to friends and neighbors.
    - Give presents to the poor—this is called *matanot la'evyonim.* We are supposed to give gifts of money on Purim and to make sure that everyone has a Purim meal.

CLASS DISCUSSION (5 minutes)

How might we go about making sure that everyone has access to a Purim meal? What are some challenges of giving money on Purim to make sure everyone has enough money to have a Purim meal?

SEND THE STUDENTS TO THE YAD CHESSED WEBSITE (10–15 minutes)

If technology in the classroom allows, do this in small groups. If not, do it with the whole class together.

- Read the home page of Yad Chessed, found at www.yadchessed.org.
- Click on the "Purim program" tab on the left and read how the program works. Discuss with the class.
- Click on other tabs and look at what else Yad Chessed does. Is it only for Purim?

If your community has a similar organization, discuss it with your students instead of Yad Chessed.

Wrapping It Up: (5–10 minutes)

There is a special name for feeding the hungry on Purim. But Purim reminds us that *ma'achil r'eivim* is really a mitzvah that we should do every day, not only on Purim. Brainstorm ways that we can make sure that people have enough to eat.

Pesach: Hakhnasat Orchim

Essential Question: How can I fulfill the mitzvah of hakhnasat orchim *at the seder by being a good guest or a good host?*

Lesson Objectives: Students will be able to:

1. Articulate ways to be a good host.
2. Articulate ways to be a good guest.
3. Appreciate the *hakhnasat orchim* element of the Pesach seder.

Getting Started: (5 minutes)

Open *haggadot* to Ha Lachma Anya. Read the paragraph in English. Focus on "Let all who are hungry, come and eat /Let all who are in need come and share the Pesach meal." How do we fulfill this mitzvah? (*give tzedakah before the holiday to make sure people can afford to make a seder; some communities have communal* s'darim *for people who prefer; most synagogues help match hosts and guests so everyone who wants will have a place to go)*

Experiential Learning: (20–30 minutes)

Pesach game to be played in small groups. Give each group the clues in a different order. When each group finishes all the activities, they are given the "afikoman" and a treat such as a chocolate bar, or a macaroon.

Activities:

- Four guests come to the seder. One asks very good questions. Prepare a question to ask at the seder. If the teacher approves the question, write it on as many index cards as there are students in your group so that each student can bring it to his/her own seder. Which guest do you think this one is? *(wise guest)* Get the next clue.
- Four guests come to the seder: a child who is rude to the host, a teenager who refuses to participate, a parent who embarrasses his/her kids, a relative who gossips loudly about family members. Put on a skit showing how these guests act and how the hosts respond. Which guest do these represent? *(wicked guest)* Get the next clue.
- Four guests come to the seder. One chooses not to be fancy or elaborate. What might this guest wear? What present might the guest bring? Do the clothes have to be fancy and does the gift have to be expensive? What might a simple host who chooses to be plain and down-to-earth be like? What might his/her house look like? Does one have to have a big, fancy house to invite guests over? Write a rap about this guest and this host. Which guest is it? *(simple guest)* Get the next clue.
- Four guests come to the seder. One is very shy. One is at a seder for the very first time. One is a stranger in a room full of people who know each other. One is embarrassed. Write a newspaper headline about this guest and how the host helps put him/her at ease. Which guest is this? *(the one who doesn't know how to ask)* Get your next clue.

Wrapping It Up: (10–15 minutes)

Come back together as a class and let each group present one of its creative activities for the others. Some of us are going to be guests at a seder this year. Some of us are having other people in our homes for a seder. There are two *s'darim;* so, some of us might be guests one night and hosts the other. What can we do to be good guests at a seder? What can we do to be good hosts at a seder?

Shavuot: Kedushah

Essential Question: How do we demonstrate the kedushah *of Torah?*

Lesson Objectives: Students will be able to:

1. Compare how we treat the Torah to how we treat people: with respect, care, and deference.
2. Define the terms: *S'frei kodesh, Limudei kodesh; Klei kodesh.*
3. Appreciate the *kedushah* of Torah as a gift from God.

Getting Started: (5–10 minutes)

- Place a *Tanach,* a *Chumash,* and a siddur next to each other on the desk. Make sure the students know what each book is.
- Tell the class that if you have to stack them, the tradition is to treat the holiest book as the best or the most important.
- Have a volunteer come up and stack the books, and then explain his/her logic in stacking them. See if someone else wants to stack them in a different order and explain his/her reasoning. *(Note: the goal here is the thought process and reasoning; we are not looking for "the right answer.")*
- Tell the class that many rabbis teach that the holiest book should be on top, so that nothing less holy rests upon it. But at least one rabbi teaches that the least holy book should be on top, so that it is the one that gets dirty while it protects the other books.

Experiential Learning: (10–15 minutes)

- Ask: How do we treat a Sefer Torah with *kedushah*? *(crown and mantle like royalty; silver breastplate like kohein; special yad; stand when it "stands"; kiss it; bury it)*
- The best way to demonstrate the holiness and importance of Torah is to study it! That is also one of the ways we celebrate Shavuot.

Exploring the Text: (10–15 minutes)

- Introduce the terms below. Note the repeated use of the word *kadosh.* What do we learn from that?
  - ***Sifrei kodesh***—holy books; refers to Torah in the broad sense, including Torah, *Tanakh,* Talmud, Midrash, books of Jewish law, *siddurim,* etc.
  - ***Limudei kodesh***—holy studies; refers to the study of any of the above
  - ***Klei kodesh***—holy vessels; refers to rabbis, cantors, and teachers of *limudei kodesh.*
- After distributing prepared study sheets with the following text, read and discuss together:
  Our sages of blessed memory warned that one should not teach law in front of one's teacher (rather, one should defer to one's teacher); similarly, one should not teach law in front of one's teacher when one's teacher is a book! Even if the matter is obvious to him, in any case, out of respect for the book, it is appropriate to open it up and to look up what is the law. For the letters themselves provide wisdom, and many times the law is made clearer from looking in the book than from just teaching from memory. (Hanhagot Tzadikim, R. Yonah Landsofer 8:45).

Wrapping It Up: (5 minutes)
In the words of Jeffrey Spitzer of Gann Academy of Waltham, MA: "Usually we give gifts to celebrate an anniversary. Shavuot is an anniversary to celebrate a gift." What is the gift?

PART 4
Family Education Programs

INTRODUCTION

Jewish family education seeks to liberate Judaism from the exclusive domain of the congregation. This idea is not as revolutionary as it might sound. Dr. Craig Dykstra, a theologian at Duke Divinity School, observes that "when the religious community uses its language simply for its own self-perpetuation, then God has been captured as the god of the religious cults and is no longer the God of all life." In other words, Jewish education must be about more than merely teaching ritual behaviors, such as how to recite *Havdalah,* or how to wave a *lulav.* It must also be about demonstrating that Judaism is relevant to every aspect of our students' lives..

Jewish Values and Family Life

In striving to find meaning in life, we define and prioritize what really matters. Torah and the codes of Jewish law provide us with the *mitzvot* (commandments) and their applications to daily life. *Mitzvot* are about ritual observance and right conduct—the do's and don'ts of living a Jewish life within a social context. Jewish values, on the other hand, might be considered as guidelines for how to carry out our deeds and how best to interact with our family, ourselves, and with God. They reflect the intentionality of our efforts and the caliber of our actions.

As an example: To carry out a deed of loving kindness has great merit. But to carry out a deed of loving kindness with *anavah* (humility) raises the level of the interaction. Another example: *Hakhnasat Orchim* literally means "bringing in guests." We can certainly fulfill this obligation by inviting people to our homes for Shabbat dinner. But how much richer our efforts become when we develop in ourselves the traits of hospitality, humility, and graciousness at all times.

How we act; who we are; what we stand for; how we respond; how we view life and the world around us; our personal qualities, attributes, traits—all these reflect the degree to which we embrace Jewish values. While they have universal application, Jewish values are an integral part of our tradition. Discussions of values and references to their importance appear in countless texts. Yet, it is more difficult to measure values than to measure other obligations. For instance, we can measure if the *shofar* is sounded on Rosh Hashanah—it either is or it isn't. In contrast, how can we measure gratitude or holiness or family harmony? Yet, without such virtues, our lives are less well-rounded, less enriched, and less complete.

The goal of the family activities section is to enable students and their families to appreciate that living Jewish values will increase their emotional, interpersonal, and spiritual lives.

FAMILY EDUCATION PROGRAMS: LESSON 1

Introduction to Living Jewish Values

Essential Question: How can Jewish values add meaning to our lives?

Introduction

Invite students' families to join your class at school for a 90-minute session when your class begins to study *Living Jewish Values.* Ask each family to bring to school any old magazines or newspapers that they have around their homes that they no longer need.

Lesson Objectives: Families will be able to:

1. Understand how Jewish values add meaning to their lives.
2. Explore where their values come from.
3. Discuss how Jewish values influence both their personal and family lives.

Experiential Learning

1. (10 minutes) Brainstorm with families a list of positive values and write them on the board. Explain that this session will explore how values add meaning to our lives.
2. (15 minutes) Family members share with their own families one value that is important and meaningful to them, and give a concrete example of how that value influences their personal lives. They may tell a story about a time when that value influenced their actions, or describe an activity that they do regularly in keeping with that value.
3. (15 minutes) Each family chooses one value that is meaningful to them and gives a concrete example of how that value influences their family life. Those families who wish can share their value and example with the rest of the class.
4. (30 minutes) Each family discusses where their family's values come from—both the personal values of each family member and their family values. Sources for their values may include people they look up to, the media, religion, texts, etc. Each family receives a poster board and makes a collage representing different sources of their family values. The teacher should provide markers; American magazines and newspapers; Jewish magazines; pictures of Jewish rituals, ritual objects, and Jewish historical events; quotes from central Jewish and American texts, etc. If members of one family have different and sometimes conflicting sources of values, they should make sure their collage represents all the different sources.
5. (10 minutes) When families are done with their collages, they can walk around the room, look at other families' collages, and ask questions about what they see.
6. (10 minutes) Bring the group together, and ask: Which items, if any, in your family's collage are Jewish? How does Judaism influence your personal and family values? Explain that as a class, you are going to explore Jewish values and how they can enrich your personal and family lives.

FAMILY EDUCATION PROGRAMS: LESSON 2

Conclusion to Living Jewish Values

Essential Question: How can Jewish values improve our family life?

Introduction

- Invite students' families to join your class at school for a 90-minute session to conclude your class's study of *Living Jewish Values.* In preparation for the session, divide your class into four groups. Each group prepares a short presentation (around 5 minutes) for one of the values that you have studied in this volume: *hakarat hatov, sh'lom bayit, emet,* and *kedushah.*
- In each presentation, the group gives the Hebrew words for their value, defines the value, and acts out a situation where a family faces a dilemma relating to that value. The skit should not include the resolution of the dilemma. Instead, the skit should end with an open-ended question about what your family would do in this situation. For example, the skit could be about a family discussing what to do during a family vacation so that the vacation includes both fun and *kedushah.* The skit ends with the question: What activities would your family include in the vacation and why?

Lesson Objectives: Families will be able to:

1. Provide examples of Jewish family values.
2. Explain how these values can influence family life.
3. Make a concrete plan for how one of these values can improve their family life.

Experiential Learning:

1. (50 minutes) Welcome the families. Explain that the class has been learning about Jewish family values, and each group of students has prepared a presentation of one of the values they have learned about. Each group then gives its presentation. After each presentation, individual families discuss among themselves how they would act in this situation. Allow 5 minutes for an introduction, 5 minutes for each skit, 5 minutes for each family discussion, and 1–2 minutes to transition from one group to the next.
2. (25 minutes) Each family chooses one of the four values that they would like to work on, and makes an action plan for how they will apply this value to their family life. Each family completes the worksheet attached.
3. (15 minutes) Those families who would like to can share their action plans with the group.

FAMILY EDUCATION PROGRAMS: WORKSHEET

How can Jewish values improve our family life?

Our family has chosen the following value to work on:

We believe this value is important because

We are going to do the following activity in order to apply this value to improve our family life:

We will start on this date:

Through this activity, we hope to achieve: